Contents

Some words are shown in bold, **like this**.
You can find them in the glossary on page 23.

What is a jellyfish?

A jellyfish is a soft-bodied sea animal.

Jellyfish live in oceans all over the world.

A Day in the Life: Sea Animals

Jellyfish

Louise Spilsbury

www.raintreepublishers.co.uk
Visit our website to find out
more information about
Raintree books.

To order:
☎ Phone 0845 6044371
🖷 Fax +44 (0) 1865 312263
🖳 Email myorders@raintreepublishers.co.uk

Customers from outside the UK please telephone +44 1865 312262

Raintree is an imprint of Capstone Global Library Limited,
a company incorporated in England and Wales having
its registered office at 7 Pilgrim Street, London, EC4V 6LB
– Registered company number: 6695582

Text © Capstone Global Library Limited 2011
First published in hardback in 2011
First published in paperback in 2012
The moral rights of the proprietor have been asserted.

Edited by Sian Smith, Nancy Dickmann, and Rebecca Rissman
Designed by Joanna Hinton-Malivoire
Picture research by Mica Brancic
Production by Victoria Fitzgerald
Originated by Capstone Global Library Ltd
Printed and bound in China by South China Printing
 Company Ltd

ISBN 978 1 4062 1702 5 (hardback)
14 13 12 11 10
10 9 8 7 6 5 4 3 2 1

ISBN 978 1 4062 1886 2 (paperback)
15 14 13 12 11
10 9 8 7 6 5 4 3 2 1

**British Library Cataloguing in Publication
Data**

Spilsbury, Louise.
   Jellyfish. -- (A day in the life. Sea animals)
   1. Jellyfishes--Pictorial works--Juvenile literature.
   I. Title II. Series
   593.5'3-dc22

Acknowledgements

We would like to thank the following for permission to
reproduce photographs: FLPA p.19 (Minden Pictures/Ingo
Arndt); Getty Images pp.18, 23: polyp (Getty Images); Image
Quest Marine pp.12, 23: bell (V&W/Mark Conlin), 13 (Peter
Parks), 17, 23: tentacle (Chris Parks), 21 (Andre Seale), 22
(Kare Telnes); Photolibrary pp.4 (WaterFrame/Underwater
Images/Franco Banfi), 5, 23: swarm (Oxford Scientific Films
(OSF)/Howard Hall), 6 (imagebroker.net/Ingo Schulz), 7 (age
fotostock/Morales Morales), 8 (Index Stock Imagery/Wayne
& Karen Brown), 9 (Corbis), 10, 23: zooplankton (Animals
Animals/Tim Rock), 11, 23: venom (Oxford Scientific Films
(OSF)/Paul Kay), 14 (WaterFrame - Underwater Images/
Franco Banfi), 15 (Tsuneo Nakamura), 16, 20, 23: sense cells
(Tips Italia/Reinhard Dirscherl).

Cover photograph of jellyfish at Monterey Bay Aquarium
reproduced with permission of Corbis (© Atlantide Phototravel/
Stefano Amantini). Back cover photograph of a swarm of moon
jellyfish reproduced with permission of Photolibrary (Oxford
Scientific Films (OSF)/Howard Hall). Back cover photograph
of tentacles reproduced with permission of Photolibrary
(imagebroker.net/Ingo Schulz).

We would like to thank Michael Bright for his invaluable help
in the preparation of this book.

swarm

There are many different types of jellyfish.

Sometimes jellyfish live in groups
called **swarms**.

What do jellyfish look like?

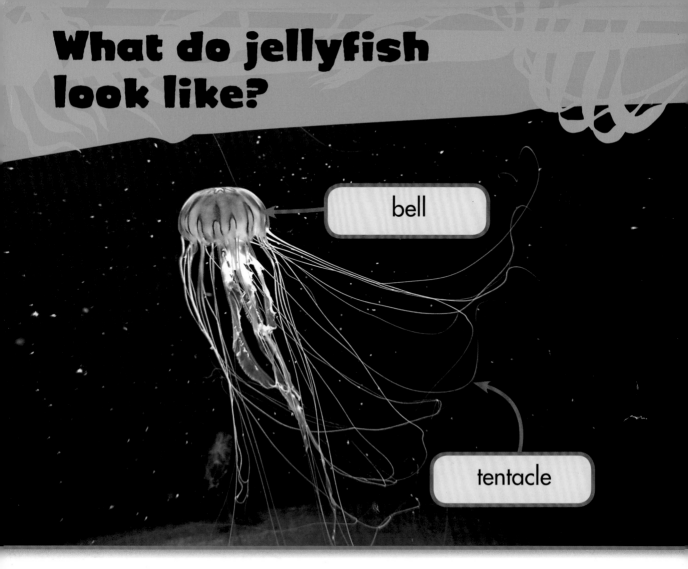

bell

tentacle

A jellyfish has a soft, round top called a **bell**.

Tentacles hang down from the bell.

ring

The moon jellyfish has a pale blue or pink bell.

A moon jellyfish has four horseshoe-shaped rings at the top of its bell.

What do jellyfish do?

Moon jellyfish stay in shallow waters near land.

They can find food near the top of the water.

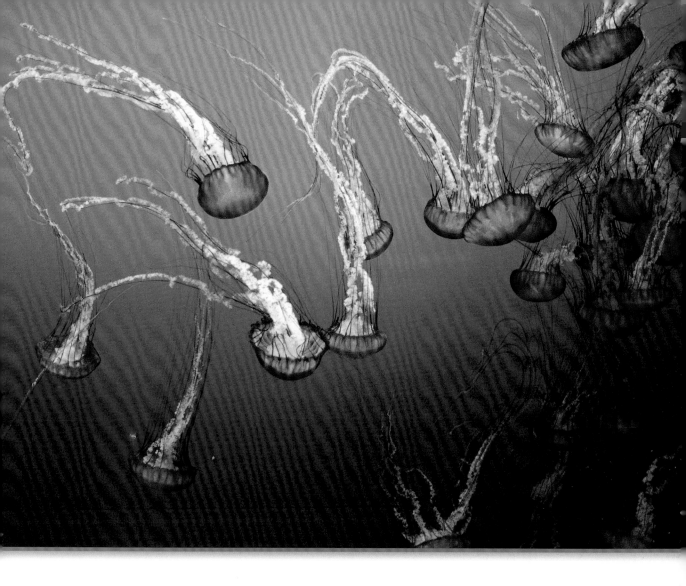

Some jellyfish move deep underwater
in the day.

At night they return to the top to
find food.

What do jellyfish eat?

zooplankton

Moon jellyfish feed on tiny **zooplankton** that float in the water.

Zooplankton includes tiny shrimp-like animals and young crabs or lobsters.

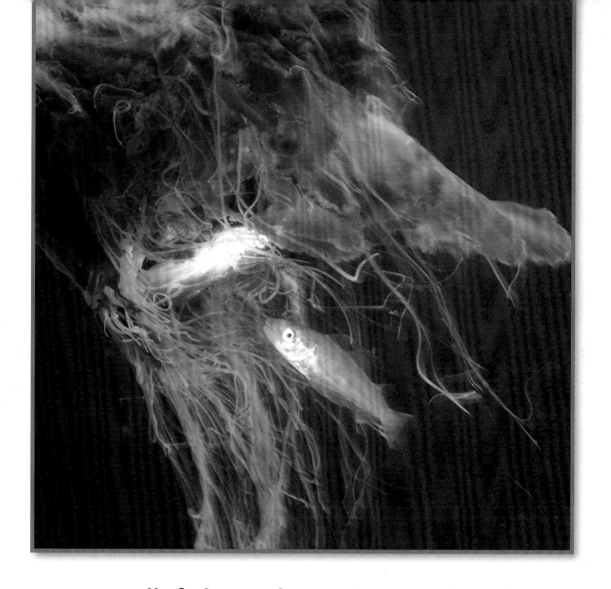

Larger jellyfish eat bigger sea animals, such as fish or shrimps.

Some jellyfish also eat other types of jellyfish!

How do jellyfish catch food?

tentacle

Jellyfish catch food with their **tentacles**.

Jellyfish have **venom** in their tentacles that stops animals moving.

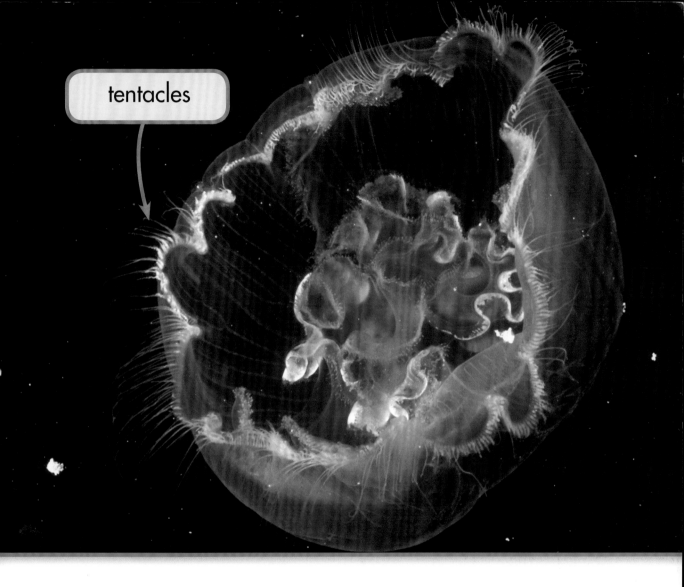

tentacles

Moon jellyfish trap food in the sticky slime on their tentacles.

Then the food is carried to the jellyfish's mouth.

How do jellyfish move?

Jellyfish travel a long way floating in the water.

The ocean carries them along as it moves.

Jellyfish can move by opening their **bell** and filling it with water.

Then they squeeze their body tight and push out the water to make them move.

Do jellyfish have senses?

Jellyfish do not have eyes or ears.

They use special **sense cells** to find their way.

Some sense cells tell jellyfish to move towards or away from light.

Jellyfish have other sense cells to smell and taste and to balance in the water.

What are jellyfish babies like?

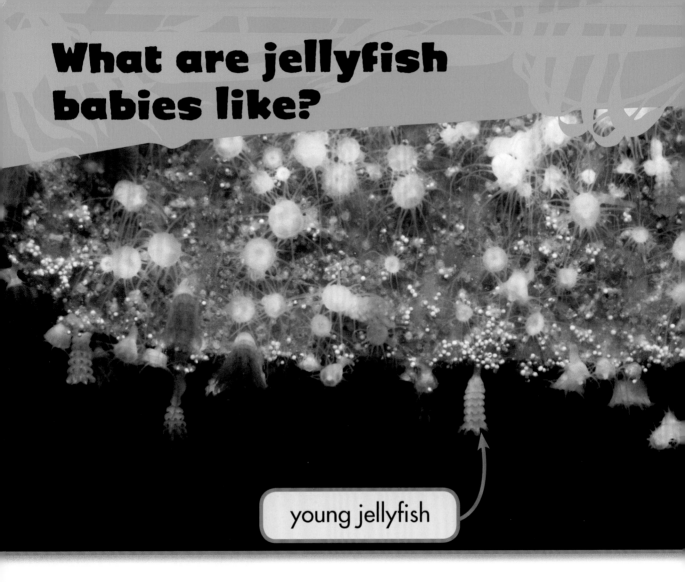

young jellyfish

Moon jellyfish eggs grow on the underside of a female's **bell**.

Young jellyfish hatch out of the eggs and stick onto rocks.

When the young jellyfish stick to rocks they are called **polyps**.

The polyps float away and some grow into adult jellyfish.

What hunts jellyfish?

turtle

Some turtles, fish, and other jellyfish hunt jellyfish.

These animals do not feel the stings from jellyfish **tentacles**.

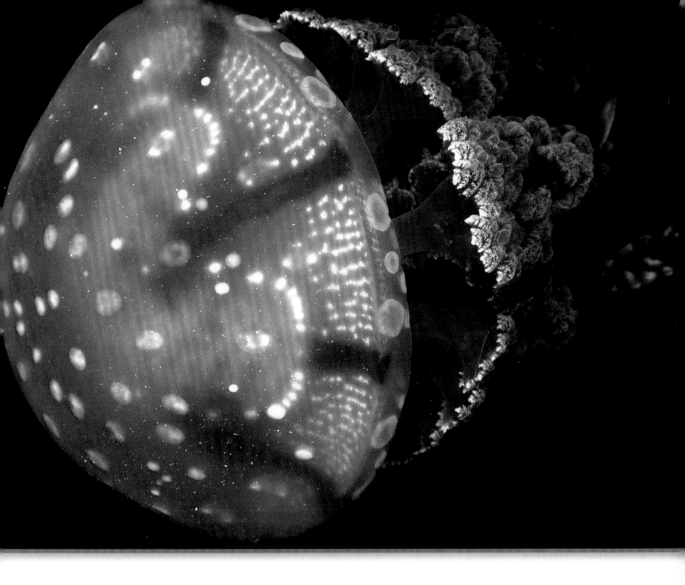

Some jellyfish start to glow if they are attacked at night!

Lights make the jellyfish look bigger to scare off its attacker.

Jellyfish body map

bell

tentacles

Glossary

bell body of a jellyfish

polyp early stage in the life of an animal such as a jellyfish

sense cells parts of a jellyfish's body that can tell the animal about the world around it

swarm group of jellyfish

tentacle long, thin part of a jellyfish's body that it uses for feeling and catching food

venom poisonous juice that can kill animals

zooplankton tiny animals that float or drift in the sea

Find out more

Books

Jellyfish (Ocean Life), Martha E. H. Rustad (Capstone Press, 2006)

Jellyfish (Scary Creatures), Gerard Cheshire (Children's Press [CT], 2008)

Websites

Watch a video on jellyfish and find out all about them at: **kids. nationalgeographic.com/Animals/CreatureFeature/Jellyfish**

For photos and facts about jellyfish go to: **news.bbc.co.uk/cbbcnews/hi/ pictures/galleries/newsid_3881000/3881353.stm**

Index